EVERYTHING SPORTS

EVERYTHING BASEBALL

SYDNEY NEWTON

A Crabtree Canopy Book

Crabtree Publishing
crabtreebooks.com

Author
Sydney Newton

Contributors
Jennifer Rivkin
Rachel Stuckey
Jaime Winters

Editors
Sissy McGonagal
Crystal Sikkens

Proofreader
Melissa Boyce

Design
Margaret Salter

Production manager
Candice Campbell

Images

Newscom: p. 34 Bill Alkofer/KRT; 35 Jose Mendez/Efe; 42 Kyodo

Wikimedia Commons: p. 6-7, 7 (circle inset), 8 (middle), 9 (bottom), 10, 11 (bottom), 12-13, 13, 14 (all) , 15 (all), 16 (all), 17, 19 (middle left), 20-21, 20, 21 (all), 22, 23 (all), 24, 25 (top and bottom), 26 (all), 27 (all), 28 (top), 29 (middle), 30, 31 (all), 32 (all), 33 (bottom and right), 36, 37 (all), 38, 39 (top left), 40 (top right and top left), 43, 44 (bottom), 45 (all), 46, 47 (top and bottom inset), 49 (top). 50, 51 (all), 52 (bottom), 53 (top and bottom left), 54, 55 (all), 57 (both), 59 (middle and bottom)

Shutterstock: p. 4 (bottom left) Alan C. Heison, 61 (top right); 49 (middle) eddtoro; front cover, 58 Debby Wong; 48 (middle) Songquan Deng; 52 (left) Photo Works; 11 (top) Joseph Sohm; 40 (bottom) Kiev.Victor; 15 (middle right inset) Matthew Dicker; 61 (bottom) Keeton Gale; 41 jazzmxx; 59 (top); 1 (middle,) 60 (left) Keeton Gale; 44 (top) ChicagoPhotographer; 56 (bottom and bottom left) Debby Wong; 9 (top) Steve Cukrov; 25 (middle) quiggyt4; 39 (bottom right) Conor P. Fitzgerald; 28 (bottom) leungchopan; 43 (left) Arthur D'Amario III; 49 (bottom) Domingo Saez; 53 (bottom right) quiggyt4; 18 (bottom) Conor P. Fitzgerald; 60 (bottom right) ChicagoPhotographer.

All other images: Shutterstock.com

Crabtree Publishing

crabtreebooks.com 800-387-7650

In Canada: We acknowledge the financial support of the Government of Canada through the Canada Book Fund for our publishing activities.

Hardcover 978-1-0398-7484-8
Ebook (pdf) 978-1-0398-8173-0
Epub 978-1-0398-8293-5

Published in Canada
Crabtree Publishing
616 Welland Avenue
St. Catharines, Ontario
L2M 5V6

Published in the United States
Crabtree Publishing
347 Fifth Avenue
Suite 1402-145
New York, NY 10016

Library and Archives Canada Cataloguing in Publication
Available at the Library and Archives Canada

Library of Congress Cataloging-in-Publication Data
Available at the Library of Congress

Printed in the U.S.A./CP072026

CONTENTS

INTRODUCTION

AMERICA'S PASTIME

The bases are loaded at the end of the inning. **Two balls and two** strikes. **The batter steps up. The pitcher winds up and releases—it's a swing and a hit. The crowd goes wild—a bases-loaded** home run!

Baseball is both a team sport and a game of individual players. It may seem slow at times, and it requires patience and skill. But it's the slow burn that keeps players playing and fans in their seats. Known as "America's **pastime**," it is a game that is also loved all over the world in countries as diverse as Australia, Canada, the Dominican Republic, Japan, Mexico, South Korea, and Taiwan. Both men and women play baseball at many different ages and levels—from **amateur** peewee to the **professional** "big leagues."

The World Baseball Classic began in 2006. This major international tournament features competing national teams from all over the world. Japan won the tournament for the third time in 2023.

Pro Baseball

Professional baseball includes Major League Baseball (MLB), as well as Minor League Baseball (MiLB), in different leagues and levels in the U.S. and Canada. There are also professional leagues throughout the world.

Teams from all over the world compete in the Little League World Series every year. The series is open to children from ages 10 to 12. It began in 1947 and has since been held every August in Pennsylvania.

CHAPTER 1

THE BIRTH OF BASEBALL

Most ancient civilizations around the world played bat-and-ball games. In Europe, some of these games evolved into cricket and rounders.

FAST FACT

In cricket, players bat the ball and run end to end to score. In rounders, a batter hits a ball thrown by a pitcher and runs around posts. The opposing team then tries to hit the batter with the ball to get the batter "out."

Ball Games

When English **settlers** arrived in North America in the 1700s, they brought the games they loved with them. Cricket didn't catch on. It could take days to play and was seen as a game for the wealthy. But rounders became popular.

Kids began playing rounders in towns all over. They used rocks, sticks, or stools for bases. During a typical game, a batter would try to hit a ball thrown by a pitcher, and then would run around the bases while trying to avoid being pounded out by the ball.

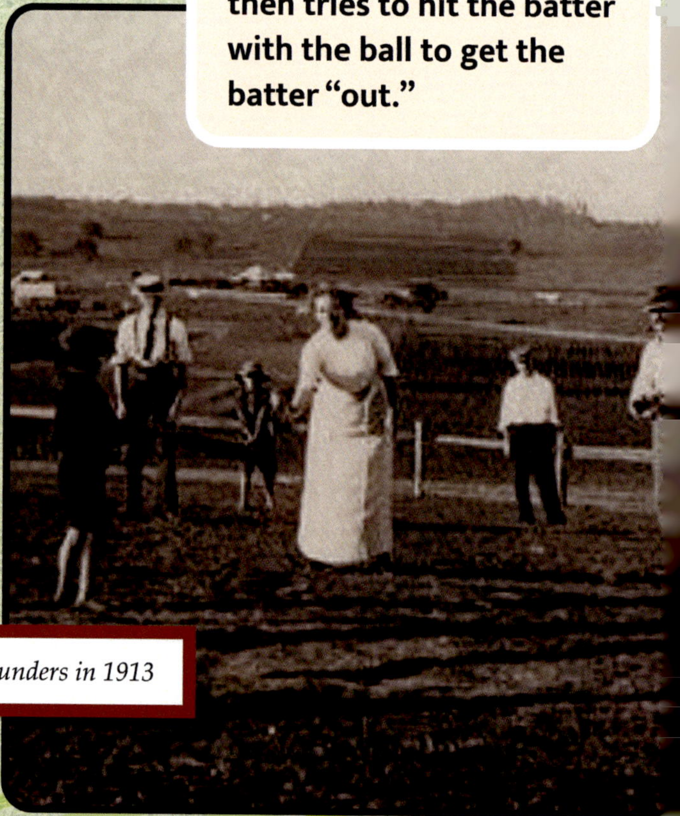

A game of rounders in 1913

Evolving Rules

The rules of rounders differed from town to town. The number of bases varied from two to five. Some towns had no teams, with just a batter playing against a mob of fielders. Others had batters try to hit a pitch that bounced off a barn wall. Town teams evolved as the game spread across the U.S.

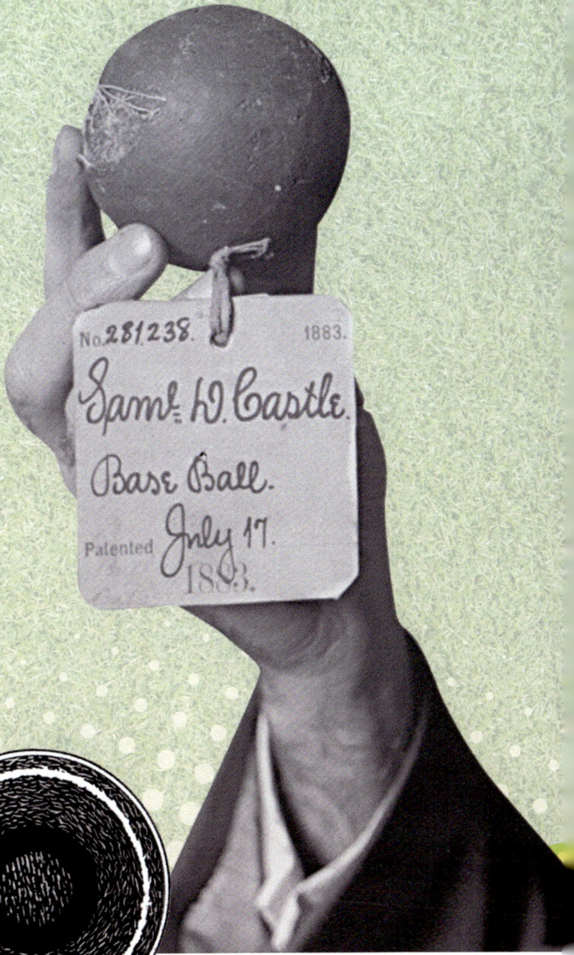

The name of rounders varied from town to town—it was called town ball, round ball, sting ball, burn ball, soak ball, stool ball, and even base ball.

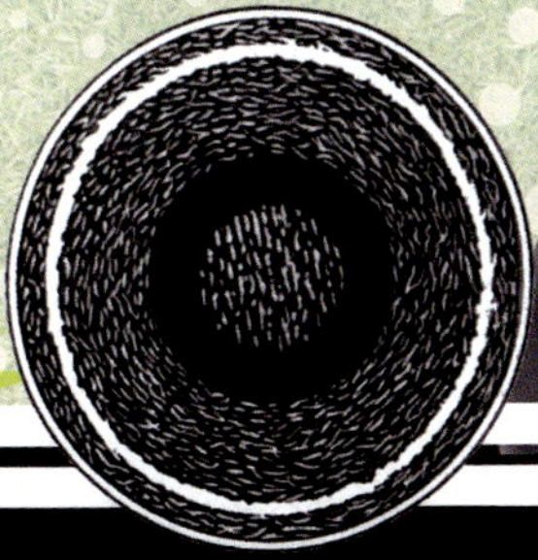

Walnuts to Rubber

Players made early balls from whatever was on hand, such as a walnut wrapped in an old sock. The balls quickly turned soft and mushy. Soon, players began winding yarn around rubber and covering it in leather. These lasted longer and traveled farther. Today, balls have a cork core wrapped in layers of rubber, wool, and cotton covered with leather.

Knickerbockers

In 1845, 25-year-old bank teller Alexander J. Cartwright started the Knickerbocker Base Ball Club of New York. Each week, Cartwright brought new rules for the club to try out at the vacant, or empty, lot where they met. He chose the rules from different versions of the game and added his own ideas. Cartwright used four bases set in a diamond shape and allowed pitchers to throw overhand rather than just underhand. Instead of **beaning** runners with the ball for an "out," Cartwright had fielders "tag" them with the ball. He wrote the rules down—and modern baseball was born. As New York City grew and became more crowded, the Knickerbockers began playing their games at the Elysian Fields in nearby Hoboken, New Jersey, in 1846.

The Knickerbockers and their rivals in 1858

Elysian Fields has since been developed and no longer has baseball diamonds. The only recreational feature left on the grounds is a small park known as Elysian Park.

Doc Adams

Daniel "Doc" Adams began playing baseball for exercise in 1839. A medical doctor, Adams joined the Knickerbocker Base Ball Club soon after it formed. He noticed that players out on the field, or outfielders, often had difficulty throwing the ball to **infielders**. He began playing **shortstop** by throwing the ball from outfielders to infielders. This closed a big gap on the field and became a regular position. Adams also designed bats and balls and helped establish the rules of the game.

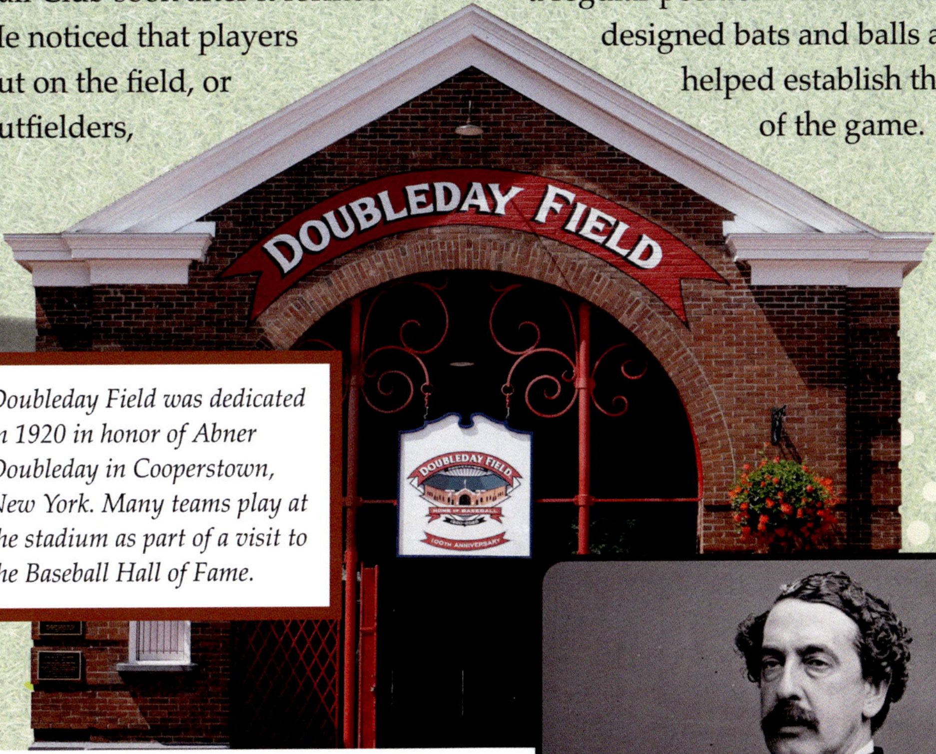

Doubleday Field was dedicated in 1920 in honor of Abner Doubleday in Cooperstown, New York. Many teams play at the stadium as part of a visit to the Baseball Hall of Fame.

Hall of Fame

Legend says that Abner Doubleday, a Union Army officer, invented baseball in 1839 in Cooperstown, New York. Doubleday never said that was true, but the myth lasted more than 90 years. Today, the National Baseball Hall of Fame and Museum is located in Cooperstown.

Rules of Order

The Knickerbocker Base Ball Club adopted Cartwright's rules in 1845. The rules made the game more exciting. They also **standardized** play and the size and shape of the field.

Standardized rules meant that competitive leagues could be formed. The appearance of leagues allowed for the growth of championship series, and the popularity of the game took off.

Cartwright's Rules

Many of Cartwright's rules are still used today. They include:

1) Run four bases to score a run.
2) A strike is a swing and a miss at the ball.
3) Three strikes is an out!
4) If the batter hits the ball, the opposing team has to catch it or throw the ball to a base for an out.
5) Three outs and the other team takes a turn at bat.
6) After nine innings for each team, the team with the most runs wins.

Baseball Fever

As clubs sprang up to challenge the Knickerbockers, baseball fever struck New York City. Huge crowds began gathering to watch the action. In 1857, more than 12 other clubs set up a rules committee and an all-star game. Soon, they formed the National Association of Base Ball Players (NABBP) to govern the game. By 1859, baseball fever swept across the Canadian border.

Crowds have been packing baseball stadiums in the New York City area for more than 150 years.

Civil War Ball

During the American Civil War (1861–1865), Union soldiers from the northeast often played baseball to let off steam behind the **front**. Fellow soldiers and Confederate prisoners watched them and learned how to play. Baseball was already being played in the southern states before the Civil War, but the returning soldiers playing on both sides helped popularize the game after the war.

All-American

As fans turned up to games in record numbers and devoured news about their favorite players, baseball quickly became the all-American game. By 1869, people wanted to take the game to the next level, and beyond New York. They also wanted to open up baseball for professional play.

In 1871, nine clubs formed the National Association of Professional Base Ball Players. It didn't last. As more and more fans paid cash for game tickets, club owners wanted in on the profits. They weren't happy with the National Association, where players made the rules and all the money. In 1876, several owners met and formed the National League (NL) to take control of the rules—and the profits. In 1901, the American League (AL) was started. In 1903, the two league champions played a postseason tournament. This later became the World Series.

The Brooklyn Atlantics got their start in 1855 and quickly became one of baseball's top clubs. They turned pro as soon as it was allowed in 1869.

The Start of the World Series

The first World Series in 1903 featured a best-of-nine games showdown between the Boston Americans and the Pittsburgh Pirates. Boston won five games to three. Huge crowds watched as the new American League champions proved that they could play as well as the National League players. The 1903 World Series was not an official tournament between the two major leagues. It was informally played between the two league champions. The World Series did not become a league-approved postseason event until 1905.

Fans packed the Polo Grounds in New York to see the Giants play in the 1905 World Series.

A Year Without

No World Series was played in 1904. The New York Giants' fiery manager had an ongoing fight with the American League president. The Giants' owner was furious with the American League for starting another team in New York. So the Giants refused to play the World Series against the American League champions. Baseball fans were outraged. The Giants took note and played the Series the next year. The Giants beat Philadelphia in five games.

Cy Young

Denton True Young was one of baseball's first Hall of Famers. Known by his nickname "Cy," Young threw the first pitch of the first World Series. The Boston star won two games to help his team defeat the Pirates. His record of 511 career wins is still baseball's best. The Cy Young Award for pitching was named in his honor.

Lou Criger was Cy Young's catcher in the first game of the 1903 World Series. He went on to catch every inning of all eight games.

CHAPTER 2

THE SPORT EVOLVES

Unlike pro athletes, amateurs are not paid to play sports. The Knickerbocker club turned down offers to go pro. Yet, some players were paid secretly or given phony jobs.

In 1876, ace pitcher Al Spalding was offered a job in Chicago as a grocery store clerk for $40 per week. The pay was about 10 times higher than the regular wage of a grocery clerk. It was added motivation to play for the Chicago White Stockings. He soon became a star pitcher and was one of the first players to use a glove. He later started a company to sell them.

SPALDING®

Al Spalding's company created the first baseball glove, American football, basketball, and volleyball. Although no longer owned by the Spalding family, the company is still a big name in sports equipment today.

From Amateur to Pro

As more and more baseball clubs formed, competition for top players became extremely fierce. Every club wanted the best players and some were prepared to pay whatever it took. In 1869, the Cincinnati Red Stockings stacked their whole team with pro players and went on a cross-country tour. They took on any challengers, winning 56 games and tying one. Other clubs then signed pros. The game itself soon turned pro as amateur clubs could no longer sign top players.

In 1879, the National League created the **reserve** clause that allowed clubs to reserve players for the next season. This gave cash-starved clubs a chance to stay competitive with rich clubs. With the reserve clause, the rich clubs couldn't lure star players away by offering them more money. But the league didn't tell the players! The reserve clause was later abolished, or ended, in 1975.

Cincinnati Red Stockings, 1869

FAST FACT

The Cincinnati Red Stockings helped make baseball a national game in the United States.

Changes to Equipment

Over the years, hammering a home run, catching a fly ball, and fielding a **grounder** have not changed much. But the equipment players use to play the game sure has. Bats used to be heavy, thick, and wooden. Today, players at all levels—except Major League Baseball—use **aluminum**, **composite**, or **hybrid** bats, which last longer than wooden ones and almost never break. MLB batters use league-approved wooden bats which must be a certain size and length. Batters have favorite brands and makes. Some use wooden "torpedo" bats that are shaped like a torpedo with a tapered end. They are thought to improve power and bat speed.

Today, batters step up to the plate wearing strong, plastic helmets to protect their heads from wild pitches. However, batting helmets did not become required gear until 1971.

No Protection

The first catchers wore no protective gear at all. In the 1870s, catchers developed masks to shield their faces from the ball. A padded mitt followed around 1889 and shin guards around 1910. Today, catchers wear a full suit of armor: a mask, helmet, neck protector, throat guard, chest protector, shin guards, and a mitt with extra padding.

In 1875, Charles Waite played first base with flesh-colored gloves, hoping no one would notice. People did and they made fun of him. But not for long! Gloves soon became standard field equipment.

Glove Science

Baseball gloves have webbing between the thumb and fingers to help catch the ball. Today, there are different types of baseball gloves for each position. Infielders use small, light gloves so they can get the ball out of their gloves quickly to make plays. Outfielders use long gloves to help them reach for fly balls. Catchers' gloves are called mitts and have lots of padding. First basemen's gloves are extra large and, like catchers', are also called mitts.

The Color Line

In the late 1800s, **racism** was **ingrained** in society. Many white people believed that Black people were inferior, or second-class. Laws and codes prevented African Americans from living in certain places, working in certain jobs, and attending schools with white people. Though there was no rule in the rule book, Black players were also shut out of Major League Baseball. This was unofficially known as the color line or color barrier. In 1887, the New York Giants wanted to sign ace pitcher George Stovey. Stovey was Black. But when Chicago superstar Cap Anson protested, the Giants backed out. Black players were **segregated** and shut out of the big leagues for the next 60 years.

Before the unwritten color line was enforced, catcher Moses Fleetwood Walker and his brother played Major League Baseball for the Toledo Blue Stockings in 1884. After 1887, African Americans didn't play again in the big leagues until 1947.

Negro Leagues

The racism of the color line forced African Americans to form their own teams and leagues. All-Black professional teams played in what was called the Negro Leagues.The Negro Leagues had some of the game's best players. Catcher Josh Gibson racked up an incredible number of career home runs. Pitcher Leroy "Satchel" Paige often had his fielders sit down while he struck out three batters in a row. Actor, athlete, and activist Paul Robeson met with the MLB **commissioner** in 1943 to appeal for integration. It was a no go. The color line remained in place until 1947. After that, the Negro Leagues began to fold, or shut down.

Josh Gibson

Leroy "Satchel" Paige

The Kansas City Monarchs and Hilldale, a Pennsylvania team, met in the first Negro World Series in 1924. The last one was played in 1948.

Trailblazers

Jackie Roosevelt Robinson led the way for African American players. He became the first Black baseball player in MLB's modern era on April 15, 1947. The star infielder played in six World Series with the Brooklyn Dodgers, helping them win in 1955. Being a first wasn't easy. Robinson endured racial abuse from fellow players and fans but fought back by playing better than his opponents. In his 10-year career, he won numerous awards, including **Rookie** of the Year in 1947. The Dodger infielder could hit, run, and field with equal skill. In his honor, every MLB team has retired his number, 42.

In 1962, Jackie Robinson was ***inducted*** *into the Baseball Hall of Fame.*

The Say Hey Kid

Known as one of the best all-around players ever, Willie Mays was a true icon of baseball. Mays started off in the Negro American League when baseball was segregated. He went on to play for the New York Giants (which later moved to San Francisco). Mays made Rookie of the Year his first season and helped his team win the National League championship. One of his plays was so outstanding that people still call it "The Catch." His 1954 over-the-shoulder running grab in center field will go down in history as one of the best fielding plays ever.

Mays was named an All-Star in 20 out of his 22 seasons and ended his career with the New York Mets.

The Deadball Era

In 1901, the ball was less lively than today, which meant it didn't travel as far and as fast. Also, it wasn't taken out of play after it turned soft and mushy. Add to that a new rule that counted foul balls as strikes, and the Deadball Era began. Suddenly pitchers could put away batters like never before. Strikeouts skyrocketed, hits plunged, and few runs were scored. Many games were low-scoring contests between pitchers. In 1910, the ball got livelier, but pitchers covered it with spit, Vaseline, and scratches to keep scores low. The Deadball Era didn't end until 1920, when spitballs, shine balls, and scuff balls were outlawed.

Baseball has been an official team sport at Princeton University since 1864. Pictured here is their team in 1901, at the beginning of of the Deadball Era.

Babe Ruth

During the Deadball Era when home runs were scarce, George Herman "Babe" Ruth often smashed the ball out of the park. From 1914 to 1935, Ruth hit the ball out of the park a record-setting 714 times. People were stunned. The previous record of the most career home runs had been only 138. When Ruth played for the Boston Red Sox from 1914 to 1919, he was the best left-handed pitcher around. The "Bambino," as he was nicknamed, helped seal three World Series victories for the Red Sox.

Ruth was one of the first members inducted into the Baseball Hall of Fame.

Home Run King

Sports Illustrated named Babe Ruth "The Greatest Baseball Player of the 20th Century." Ruth held 56 major league records when he retired from baseball, including total bases in a season and highest hitting percentage for a season. But Ruth may be best known for the number of home runs he hit—714. His record stood for almost 40 years, until Hank Aaron broke it in 1974.

The Bambino Curse

In 1919, the Red Sox sold Babe Ruth to the New York Yankees. The Yankees went on to win the Series many times, and the Red Sox fell under the "Curse of the Bambino" for selling the All-Star player. They didn't win the World Series again until 2004, 86 years later.

When the ball got livelier in 1920, the Bambino began hitting more homers. Ruth's amazing hits helped the Yankees win. His home runs brought fans to the Yankees' ballpark. Soon the Yankees had more fans than the New York Giants, who were the owners of the ballpark where the Yankees played. Ruth hit 54 home runs in 1920, the year he arrived, and 59 in 1921. Then in 1927, he hit 60 home runs, setting a new record that lasted for many years.

Babe Ruth started in baseball as a record-setting pitcher for the Red Sox, but he wanted to play more often and became an outfielder instead.

New York Rivalry

From 1921 to 1923, the Yankees and the Giants battled in the World Series three years in a row. The Giants won the first two Series, and the Yankees took the third. After winning in 1921, the Giants kicked the Yankees out of the ballpark they owned that was home to both teams. The Yankees built a bigger ballpark, which fans called the "House that Ruth Built." They moved in 1923—the year they finally won the World Series against the Giants!

Babe Ruth ended his career with the Yankees in 1934 when he signed with the Boston Braves. He only played with the Braves for a few months before retiring in May of 1935.

The arrival of Babe Ruth made the Yankees a powerhouse in baseball. He won four more World Series and set many hitting records as a Yankee.

An International Game

Once baseball fever hit North America, it wasn't long before countries around the world caught the baseball bug too. As players traveled around the world, they took the game with them. Around 1872, American Horace Wilson was teaching in Japan. Wilson had played baseball, perhaps when he served in the American Civil War. He thought his students needed more exercise, so he taught them how to play baseball. The game caught on and a few years later Japan had its first ball team.

Horace Wilson

Today, Major League Baseball includes players that come from baseball hot spots around the world, such as Japan, Korea, Cuba, Mexico, Taiwan, Australia, and Canada.

The Taoyuan International Baseball Stadium is located in Taiwan.

World Baseball Classic

In 1938, the International Baseball Federation formed and 16 countries joined. Today, more than 100 countries belong. Countries go to bat against each other in the World Baseball Classic, held every four years. Teams feature players from leagues around the world, including Major League Baseball. The tournament takes place in the spring so that major league players can compete for their countries during MLB's off-season. Games are played in several countries. Finals take place in the United States. Top teams have come from the U.S., Japan, Korea, and Cuba.

Team USA won the bronze medal at the 2008 Olympics, finishing behind South Korea and Cuba.

Olympic Ball

From 1992 to 2008, baseball was an Olympic sport in which countries competed for medals. Players and fans were disappointed when the International Olympic Committee voted the sport out of the Games in 2012 and 2016. It made a comeback in 2020 and is scheduled to be part of the 2028 Olympics.

CHAPTER 3

WAR, WOMEN, AND CHANGE

Baseball is a sport that has adapted to many changes and challenges. One of these was World War II (1939–1945). After the United States joined the war in December 1941, many players left to serve in the armed forces.

FAST FACT

President Franklin D. Roosevelt said it was "best for the country to keep baseball going." He felt people would need to take their minds off the war.

War Years

The game went on. Players who went off to war were replaced with underage players, older players who came out of retirement, and those who were exempt from military service due to medical or physical conditions. Women's baseball became more popular as a spectator sport.

Pete Gray lost his arm in a childhood accident. In 1945, he got the opportunity to play outfielder for 77 games for the St. Louis Browns!

Not the Same Game

Nothing was the same during the war—not the hits, not the pitching, not even the ball. Without the game's top players, the quality of play dropped. So did the quality of the ball. All the good yarn went into army blankets and other war items. The ball didn't travel as far then, and home runs became tougher to hit. Clubs began using relief pitchers partway through games to try to fix their pitching difficulties.

All-Star player Joe DiMaggio played his entire career for the New York Yankees. He set an MLB record by getting a hit in 56 straight games in 1941. In 1943, DiMaggio enlisted in the army and served for just over two years.

First Pitch

Franklin D. Roosevelt, who was president during World War II, kept the tradition of throwing out a first pitch every season. Each president since 1910 has tossed at least one ceremonial first pitch.

The Beautiful Lady
BASE BALL PLAYERS
Athletes, Acrobats and Pedestrians
Blondes vs. Brunettes!
Novel, Chaste and Delightful Performances!
Under the auspices of the
National Amusement Association!
Will give one of their unparalleled performances on
Monday, Sept. 13,
AT THREE O'CLOCK, P. M.,
On the ground west of the I., B. & W. R. R.
ADMISSION—Fifty and twenty-five cts.

Women Step Up

Women have been playing baseball for as long as men, but have not had the same opportunities to play professionally. An 1875 women's game between teams called the "Blondes" and the "Brunettes" marked the first time female players were paid. During the early 1900s, women's baseball teams traveled across the United States and challenged local men's teams to games. The women's teams had strong players, but their games were considered "shows" rather than athletic events.

The New York Female Giants baseball team in 1913

League of Their Own

By 1943, baseball's biggest stars were missing in major league action due to World War II. Club owners were looking for a spark to bring fans back into the ballpark. So Chicago Cubs owner Philip Wrigley sent scouts to softball leagues in the United States and Canada to start the All-American Girls Professional Baseball League (AAGPBL). From 1943–1954, the league had 10 teams and more than 600 players. The rules were tweaked to give batters an edge over pitchers, and stealing bases was allowed. That way, big hits and exciting plays would hopefully draw fans to see rip-roaring games. And they did. About 200,000 spectators turned out to watch the games. In 1944, the league traded its softball for a hardball, gave pitchers the greenlight to throw the ball overhand, and changed its name to the All-American Girls Baseball League.

Softballs are larger than baseballs, but not actually softer. The ball is pitched underhand in a style called the windmill.

Youngest Player

Dorothy "Dottie" Schroeder was only 15 when she became the youngest player in the All-American Girls Professional Baseball League. She was the only player to play in all of the league's seasons from 1943 through 1954.

New Baseball Order

The All-American Girls Baseball League folded in 1954. Ladies League Baseball (LLB) started in 1997 and folded in 1998. Today, women's and girls' ball leagues include teeball, softball, and fast-pitch softball. The Women's Pro Baseball League (WPBL) began tryouts in 2025 for its first season in 2026. It was co-founded by Justine Seigal, the first woman to coach a professional men's team. Seigal also coached the first all-girls' team to compete in a national boys' tournament in 2002.

In 1998, Ila Borders became the first woman to win a men's pro baseball game. She pitched six shutout innings for the minor league Duluth-Superior Dukes of Minnesota to beat the Sioux Falls Canaries.

Baseball as a Living

Many women play pro and semi-pro ball for a living. Many also have full-time and part-time jobs as trainers, coaches, and managers. Eri Yoshida is a pitcher in the Empire Professional Baseball League (EPBL), an American professional league based in New York state. At age 16, she became the first woman **drafted** by a men's league in Japan. Yoshida's knuckleball with sidearm delivery earned her the nickname the "Knuckleball Princess." When she was 12, Victoria Ruelas made history as the first American girl to play in the Little League World Series. She went on to play college softball and competed in the 2001 Women's World Series. Ayami Sato is a pitcher in the semi-pro Intercounty Baseball League in Canada. She was a starter on Japan's women's national team and led them to five World Cup medals with her 80 mile-per-hour (129 kph) throw.

Women's baseball was included for the first time in the 2015 Pan Am Games in Toronto, Ontario.

World Cup

The Women's Baseball World Cup is an international tournament for women's national baseball teams. It has been held every two years since 2004. When Japan and the U.S. played for the gold medal at the 2014 Women's Baseball World Cup, Japan won hands down. The team thrashed the Americans 3–0 to claim their fourth World Cup in a row. Japan's team has dominated the Women's Baseball World Cup, winning every gold medal since 2008.

CHAPTER 4

MOVING AND EXPANDING

After World War II, fans flocked to ballparks in record numbers. From 1945–1949, attendance almost doubled from 10.8 million to 20 million.

Big Moves

After the 1957 season, the New York Giants and the Brooklyn Dodgers moved west in search of greater profits. Their fierce **rivalry** came with them. The Giants staked out San Francisco and the Dodgers made Los Angeles their new home field. Just two years later, the Dodgers won the World Series against the Chicago White Sox.

FAST FACT

Baseball's popularity kept growing in the post-war years. This was aided by games on the radio, the ease of air travel, and the growing popularity of television in the 1950s.

Major League Baseball on television became popular in the 1950s as more people could afford TVs. All major TV networks aired baseball games.

Baseball Expands

In 1961, MLB expanded when the Washington Senators moved to Minnesota and became the Minnesota Twins. A new team was founded in Washington under the old Senators name. The Los Angeles Angels also set up in Anaheim, California. In 1965, they became known as the California Angels, then the Anaheim Angels. The club name is now again officially the Los Angeles Angels.

Actor Gene Autry (1907–1998), known as "the singing cowboy," was the founding owner of the Los Angeles Angels from 1961–1997. When the Angels won the World Series in 2002, Autry was honored with the playing of his hit song "Back in the Saddle Again."

Sandy Koufax holds up four balls with zeros on them, one for each of his no-hitters.

Game Changers

By 1963, MLB thought hitting home runs had become too easy. So they enlarged the strike zone to give pitchers more room to work with. Not only did home runs drop, but so did hits. Strikeouts soared and pitchers began to rule the field once more. In particular, hurler Sandy Koufax led the Los Angeles Dodgers to victory in the 1963 World Series. By 1968, MLB reduced the strike zone to take back a pitcher's edge. It also lowered the pitching mound!

Shifts and Moves

Since 1961, Major League Baseball has continued to expand in North America. There are now 30 teams, divided equally between the National and American Leagues. In the 1969 expansion, four new teams joined—two in the National League and two in the American League. The National League additions included the San Diego Padres in southwest California and the Montreal Expos in Quebec—the first team in Canada. Even though the Expos lost 20 games in a row in their first season, they were an instant hit. Local fans soon called them "Nos Amours," which is French for "our beloved."

The Expos ended their run in Montreal in 2004—moving to Washington, D.C., and becoming the Washington Nationals. American League additions in 1969 were the Kansas City Royals and the Seattle Pilots.

Baseball expanded partly to remain competitive in a growing sports market where the National Football League (NFL) was competing for fan attention. In 1969, the National and American Leagues split into two divisions each—East and West—for a total of four divisions.

U.S. President Richard Nixon threw out the first pitch in the opening day game between the Washington Senators and the New York Yankees in 1969.

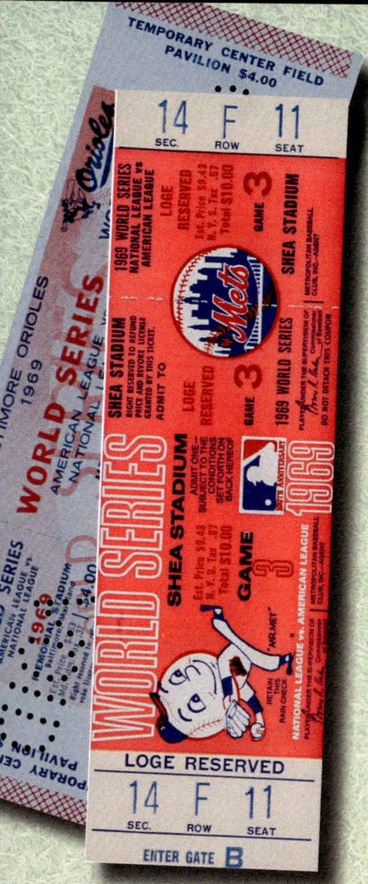

Pennant and Series

Each year, pennant winners, or playoff champs in the National League and the American League, battle it out in the World Series. The first World Series was held in 1903. It is also called the Fall Classic, as it is takes place in October. Early on, the Series had scandals. This included one in 1919 where several Chicago White Sox players were accused of deliberately losing, or "throwing" the Series for money. The players were banned for life. They never captured another Series until 2004. Some baseball **dynasties** have made their marks as World Series record holders. The New York Yankees have won 27 World Series— more than any other MLB team.

New Position

In 1973, scoring was low in the American League. So was the number of fans in ballparks. To increase both, the American League created the position of designated hitter (DH). The DH bats instead of the pitcher. This was different from the National League, and wasn't used in the World Series until 1976—but then only in even-numbered years. Sound confusing? It was. In 1986, MLB decided to use the DH rule in all World Series games played in American League teams' ballparks. In 2022, the National League adopted the DH, making it a universal rule throughout MLB.

Later Expansions

The 1977 expansion brought the Seattle Mariners to Seattle, Washington. This was another team owned, in part, by a Hollywood star: Danny Kaye. They clinched divisional titles in 1995 and 1997. The expansion also brought another team to Canada. The Toronto Blue Jays are the only non-American team in Major League Baseball today. In 1992, the Jays placed first in their division, captured the pennant, and defeated the Atlanta Braves in the World Series. In 1993, the team won the Series again!

Movie star Danny Kaye co-owned the Mariners from 1976–1981.

Ken Griffey Jr. played most of his 22-year career with the Seattle Mariners. He is considered one of the greatest baseball players of all time.

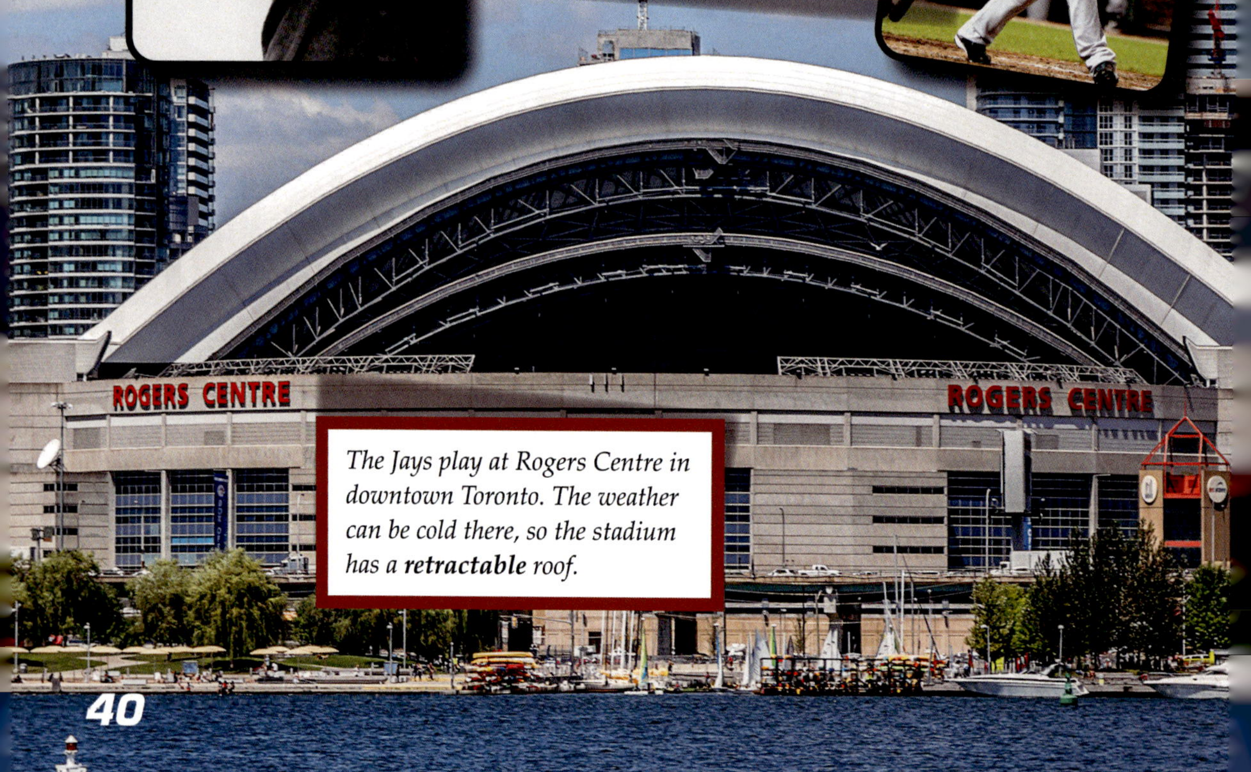

The Jays play at Rogers Centre in downtown Toronto. The weather can be cold there, so the stadium has a ***retractable*** *roof.*

More Teams

In the 1990s, MLB added more teams. It also created a new division in each league—the Central division. This meant that three teams in each league advanced to the playoffs to determine who would represent the league in the World Series. The team with the best win-loss record that didn't win a division also advanced to the playoffs. This team is known as the **wild card** team. In 2022, a new playoff format was introduced in which six teams from each league—the three division winners and three wild card teams—advanced to the playoffs.

There have only been three years in which both teams in the World Series were wild card teams. In 2023, the wild card teams Arizona Diamondbacks and Texas Rangers competed for the World Series championship. The Rangers won the series in five games. The Los Angeles Dodgers were a wild card team that won the Series in 2025.

In 1991, the Toronto Blue Jays became the first MLB club to draw more than 4 million fans to its home games in just one season.

The World Series

The team that wins the World Series is deemed the best baseball team in the world. When a team wins the Series, the ballpark erupts in joy and chaos. The winning team receives the Commissioner's Trophy. The trophy is a silver baseball surrounded by 30 gold-plated flags—one for each MLB team. Home teams receive the trophy in a ceremony on the field, while visiting teams typically receive the trophy in the clubhouse. The team gets to keep the trophy, as a new one is made every year. Each team member also receives a World Series ring.

In wild card action, the Rangers defeated the Diamondbacks four games to one in the 2023 World Series. This was the Rangers first World Series win.

Series MVP

Sports reporters and MLB's top brass choose the World Series Most Valuable Player (MVP)—the player who made the most meaningful contribution to the team's performance. Home-run king Reggie Jackson won the MVP award not once but twice for clutch hitting in the 1973 and 1977 World Series.

Reggie Jackson

Madison Bumgarner won the World Series MVP award in 2014 for stellar pitching that held opponents scoreless.

The Numbers

Today, there are 30 major league clubs—29 in the U.S. and one in Canada. Fifteen belong to the National League and 15 to the American League. At the end of the season, the top six clubs in each league advance to a tournament. The tournament determines a champion in each league. The champions from each league then advance to the World Series—a best-of-seven game championship. Winning the World Series is the top feat and honor in all of baseball.

CHAPTER 5

ALL-STARS AND FAMOUS FIELDS

Every year in July, MLB takes a break midway through the season for the All-Star Game, also known as the Midsummer Classic. Top and favorite players from the National and American Leagues face off.

FAST FACT

The 2008 All-Star Game is the longest All-Star Game in history, at four hours and 50 minutes. It ran for 15 innings, with the American League winning 4–3.

Fan Faves

The All-Star Game is usually played on the second or third Tuesday in July. Fans select All-Star infielders, while managers select pitchers. Players and managers select reserves. Fans used to have more say, but in 1957, Cincinnati Reds' fans stuffed the ballot box, selecting seven players. This led to many, and continuing, rule changes to try to ensure fairness. Today, starting-position players are selected through fan voting. Players vote in nine positions plus five starting pitchers and relievers. The rest of the team is selected via the MLB commissioner's office. Players not selected for the two teams get a break in the middle of their season.

Willie Mays is often called the greatest All-Star of them all. He played in 24 All-Star Games and holds the record for runs (20), hits (23), and steals (6). He was the All-Star MVP in 1963 and 1968.

In the Beginning

The first All-Star Game was played on July 6, 1933, in Chicago. It was put on as part of the 1933 World's Fair, an event that promoted the city during the **Great Depression**, when times were tough. It was such a success that it continued. Many of baseball's greatest players have been selected to All-Star teams over the years, but the rule that each MLB team must have at least one player selected for its league's All-Star team means that many superstars don't make it.

Fans lined up around Briggs Stadium to see the 1951 All-Star Game.

All-Star's Greatests

The Ted Williams Most Valuable Player Award, previously called the Arch Ward Memorial Award and the Commissioner's Trophy, has been presented to the most outstanding All-Star player each year since 1962. Trophy winners include superstars such as Willie Mays, Steve Garvey, Gary Carter, Cal Ripken Jr., and Mike Trout, who all won it twice. Some years, the award was shared by two players. In others, the award was won by players whose team lost the game, including father and son Ken Griffey Sr. and Ken Griffey Jr.

Ted Williams was a left fielder who played for the Boston Red Sox (1939–1960).

Out of the Park!

In 2007, Ichiro Suzuki made All-Star history when he walloped a fastball up, up, and away. In most parks, the ball would have sailed into the stands to be scooped up by some lucky fan. But not in San Francisco's wonky ballpark. The ball bounced weirdly off the center-field wall. By the time outfielder Ken Griffey Jr. got his glove on it, Ichiro was rounding third base on his way to home plate. Ichiro scored the first inside-the-park home run in an All-Star Game.

In 2000, Derek Jeter won both the All-Star Game MVP and the World Series MVP in the same year.

Home Run Derby

MLB added the Home Run Derby to the All-Star Game events in 1985, and it has been growing in popularity ever since. The slugging contest is held the day before the All-Star Game. Millions of people watch on TV to see which player will hit the most home runs. Four sluggers from each league are chosen to compete in the event. Usually they are

Famous Fields

There are 30 baseball "parks" or stadiums used by MLB teams. Most are modern and built to seat crowds of 40,000 to 56,000 on multiple levels. Fenway Park in Boston, Massachusetts, is the oldest. It's been the home field of the Boston Red Sox since 1912. Its left-field wall, nicknamed the Green Monster, or just "the wall," is legendary. At 37.2 feet (11.33 m) high, it is the highest in MLB. The wall is **infamous** for preventing home runs on line drives. Not only can it stop surefire hits from flying over the fence, but it can also swat them back where fielders least expect. One vintage monster moment was the 12th inning of Game 6 of the 1975 World Series. Red Sox catcher Carlton Fisk whacked the ball up and over the Green Monster. The home run won Game 6 for the Red Sox. Fisk's knowledge of the wall and hitting ability won the day.

Fenway Park is the oldest MLB ballpark.

Yankee Stadium

In 1922, the New York Yankees began building a new ballpark. They designed it to favor left-handed hitters, particularly their slugging superstar Babe Ruth. The plan worked. When Yankee Stadium opened, the right center bleachers were soon called "Ruthville," because Ruth hit so many homers that landed there. The stadium not only helped carry Babe to success, but also the Yankees. Babe went on to hit record numbers of home runs in the World Series, leading the Yankees to win more World Series than any other team. In 2009, the Yankees moved to their brand-new stadium just across the street. The outside was built to look like the original, but the inside has modern updates, such as roomier seats. They won the 2009 World Series against the Philadelphia Phillies in six games that year.

The original Yankee Stadium was demolished, or torn down, in 2010.

CHAPTER 6

BIG SHOTS AND HOTSHOTS

Baseball is a game of characters—each with their own skills, talents, and personalities. Some characters are players, some are officials, and others are managers, coaches, and owners.

Top Brass

MLB is the world's top professional baseball league. It is also a big business run by a commissioner chosen by team owners. Owners are wealthy business people. Teams are valued in multiple billions of dollars. Some teams are owned by family businesses. The first commissioner (1920–1944) was Kenesaw Mountain Landis, a judge, legal scholar, and baseball fan. He was known for being tough on eight big-name early players who fixed games in the 1919 World Series. Landis refused to **reinstate** them to play. They were only reinstated in 2025 by commissioner Rob Manfred—long after they were all dead. The reinstatement honored their skills and allowed them to be eligible for Hall of Fame induction.

FAST FACT

MLB is known for its colorful team owners, managers, coaches, and players. Legendary catcher, manager, and coach Yogi Berra was known for his funny statements, or "Yogi-isms," such as "It ain't over 'til it's over."

"Shoeless Joe" Jackson was a batting superstar in 1919 when his career came to an early end after he and seven other players were found to have thrown the 1919 World Series for money.

Managers and Coaches

Baseball managers make sure the teams function day to day. They do a number of things, including overseeing finances, acting as go-betweens with owners, and setting up strategy. Most of the greatest managers and coaches of all time were once top players.

Joe McCarthy

Joe McCarthy managed the New York Yankees from 1931 to 1946 during their "Bronx Bombers" years. He won seven World Series championships—tied for the most with Casey Stengel. McCarthy's "Ten Commandments for Success in the Majors" included a simple rule: do not quit. In the modern era of MLB, Sparky Anderson was the first manager to win World Series in both the American and National Leagues. He was known for his leadership and praise of players.

Buck O'Neil was the first Black coach and manager in MLB. He was also a manager in the Negro Leagues. He was inducted into the Baseball Hall of Fame in 2022.

Fantastic Catchers

Crouching behind home plate to catch pitches and throwing out runners are the most observable tasks of a catcher, but it's what spectators can't see that is this position's most important job. Catchers, who have a view of the entire baseball diamond, direct defensive play and recommend throws using hand signals for the pitcher.

San Francisco Giants catcher Buster Posey had a remarkable MLB career. He won the National League Rookie of the Year in 2010. That same year, he won his first World Series ring, and went on to win two more in 2012 and 2014. Posey's rise to the top had a few bumps. In 2011, after a collision at home plate, he was left with an injured ankle. He made a comeback in 2012—as the National League's batting champion, MVP, and Comeback Player of the Year! Posey retired from playing baseball in 2021.

Posey's last game was in October 2021. He spent his 12-year professional career with the San Francisco Giants.

Yadier Molina

Yadier Molina was called up to the majors to play for the St. Louis Cardinals in 2004. He is known for throwing out runners attempting to steal bases and for directing defensive play. He helped his team win two World Series in 2006 and 2011, and has won nine Rawlings Gold Glove Awards for defensive play.

Yogi Berra of the New York Yankees was one of the greatest catchers in baseball history. He was inducted into the Baseball Hall of Fame in 1972.

On the Mound

The best pitchers are both powerful and smart. They know what pitch to use depending on the batter, the team, and the score of a game. To prevent the batter from connecting with the ball, pitchers throw a variety of pitches, such as fastballs, curveballs, knuckleballs, and sliders.

Nolan Ryan

Eight-time All-Star Nolan Ryan's accomplishments are legendary. He's an all-time leader in no-hitters, with seven in his 27-year career—three more than any other pitcher. Ryan holds the MLB record with 5,714 strikeouts—having notched 300 strikeouts in a season six different times! He also ranks first for the fewest hits allowed per nine innings (6.56). The Texas native played for the New York Mets, California Angels, Houston Astros, and Texas Rangers.

Shohei Ohtani

With a nickname like "Shotime," Shohei Ohtani has proved to be quite a performer. The Japanese pitcher and designated hitter has also been compared to Babe Ruth. He played in Nippon Professional Baseball in Japan before joining the Los Angeles Angels in 2018, and was named American League Rookie of the Year. He became the first to earn at least 37 home runs and 15 stolen bases by mid-season—proving his batting skills in addition to pitching. It earned him another MVP award—the first DH to win the award. He also earned two Guinness World Records. He joined the L.A. Dodgers in 2024, signing a $700 million contract—the largest in professional sports history at the time.

Shohei Ohtani helped the Dodgers win back-to-back World Series titles in 2024 and 2025. He won National League MVP both years.

Clayton Kershaw

When L.A. Dodgers' starting pitcher Clayton Kershaw played his first major league game in 2008, he was just 20 years old—and the youngest player in MLB at the time. Kershaw quickly racked up the stats and awards. Now considered one of the greatest pitchers in MLB history, Kershaw has earned multiple awards, including a pitching Triple Crown (2011), three MLB Players' Choice National League Outstanding Pitcher Awards, and three Cy Young Awards. He added a Branch Rickey Award for community service in 2013 after opening an orphanage. Kershaw retired in 2025.

Clayton Kershaw

Hall of Fame shortstop Ozzie "The Wizard of Oz" Smith was one of the best defensive players of all time. He won 13 Gold Glove Awards for his efforts in the field during his 19-year career, and set many MLB records along the way.

Incredible Infielders

Many balls are hit to the infield, so a baseball team depends on good defense by its infielders. The four defensive players in the infield—first, second, and third base, along with shortstop—are responsible for plays on or near their bases. Superstar infielders can anticipate where a ball will end up and have quick reaction times. They are great at catching and have the ability to throw both powerfully and accurately.

Derek Jeter

Derek Jeter was drafted out of high school by the New York Yankees in 1992. A shortstop, he spent his entire MLB career with one team. In his first full season in the majors in 1996, Jeter helped the Yankees win the World Series against the Braves. He won the American League Rookie of the Year award. He went on to win four more World Series rings, was World Series MVP in 2000, and was named team captain in 2003. Among his many awards, Jeter also won five Gold Gloves for excellence at shortstop and five Silver Sluggers for his batting skill. Jeter retired in 2014, but is still so famous that even people who don't follow baseball recognize his name. That's partly because of his appearances on non-sports television shows, a documentary about his life, and his work as a sports analyst.

Derek Jeter

Family Affair

MLB is a family affair for some. There have been many fathers whose sons have followed them into the big leagues. Some have even played together. Cecil Fielder was a first baseman and DH for four teams from 1985 to 1998. His son, Prince, also played first base and was a DH for three MLB teams (2005–2016). The Fielders are the only father-son duo to hit 50 home runs in a season.

Cal Ripken Sr.

Cal Ripken Sr. was a minor and major league coach. His sons Cal Jr. and Billy played shortstop and third base throughout their MLB careers. Cal Jr. was nicknamed "The Iron Man." He won two Gold Gloves, eight Silver Sluggers, and was an All-Star 19 times! In retirement he has been owner of three minor league teams and a minority owner of the Baltimore Orioles.

Rod Carew

Rod Carew played as an MLB second baseman, first baseman, and designated hitter from 1967–1985. He was a seven-time American League batting champion and played in 18 consecutive All-Star Games. Carew was inducted into the Hall of Fame in 1991.

Outstanding Outfielders

Outfielders must catch or stop the balls that get past the infield. There are three outfielders on the field. Left, center, and right fielders try to catch long fly balls or retrieve ones that have landed and throw them back to an infielder as quickly as possible. Superstar outfielders can read the ball's path and have the speed and agility to get to it. They also need powerful and accurate throwing arms.

Mike Trout

Mike Trout is considered one of the greatest modern-era players. He exploded into MLB in 2012 as a center fielder for the Los Angeles Angels. Trout led the league in runs and times on base four times. He earned the American League Rookie of the Year award, nine Silver Sluggers, two Hank Aaron Awards, and was the American League's MVP three times. In 2019, Trout signed a 12-year contract for $426 million with the Angels. This was one of the largest sports contracts in North American history.

Trout was captain of the United States national team during the World Baseball Classic in 2023. The U.S. was defeated by Japan 3–2 in the championship game.

Amazing Hitters

Miguel "Miggy" Cabrera is considered one of the greatest hitters and defensemen of all time. In 2012, Cabrera became the first player in 45 years to win the Triple Crown in batting, which meant that the Detroit Tiger led the league in batting average, home runs, and RBIs. The Venezuelan native retired in 2023.

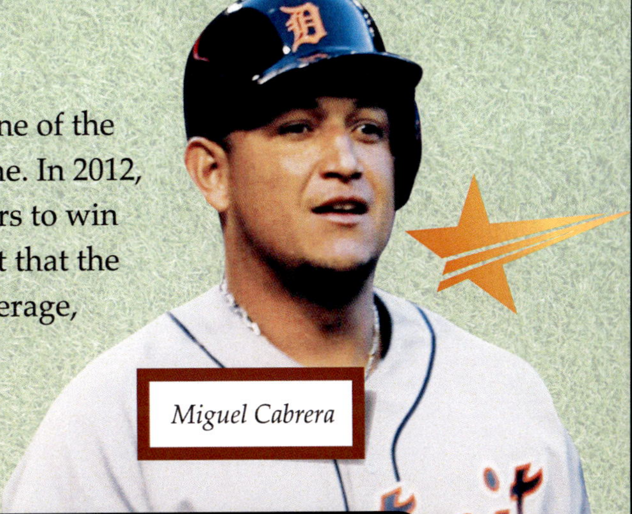

Miguel Cabrera

From 2010–2015, José Bautista had the most home runs of anyone in MLB. Nicknamed "Joey Bats," not only could the right fielder hit, winning three Silver Sluggers, but he was also outstanding in infield and outfield play. A native of the Dominican Republic, Bautista formally retired in 2023.

José Bautista

Hammerin' Hank

In 1957, right fielder Hank Aaron was the National League MVP and helped the Milwaukee Braves take home their first World Series in 43 years. In 1974, Aaron broke Babe Ruth's home run record (714). Aaron's record of 755 home runs stood until 2007. In 1999, MLB honored Aaron by introducing the Hank Aaron Award, given annually to the top hitter in each league.

Giving Back

Starting his baseball career in 2009 with 108 games, the powerful Pittsburgh Pirates center fielder Andrew "Cutch" McCutchen played his first full major league season in 2010. He has made a name for himself, winning four Silver Sluggers, an MVP award, a Gold Glove for his efforts at center field, and Wilson Defensive Player of the Year (2012). Though he stands out as a player, Andrew McCutchen is known for putting others—including his teammates and his community—first. He works with Habitat for Humanity and founded Cutch's Crew, which mentors young inner-city baseball players.

The Rawlings Gold Glove Award was given to McCutchen in 2012. It is awarded to players who show superior fielding skills.

Just "Ichiro"

Ichiro Suzuki was the only MLB player to wear his first name on his baseball jersey. The outfielder, who started training with his father at age three, played pro baseball in Japan before he joined the Seattle Mariners in 2001. Ichiro quickly showed America what he had already proven to Japan—he was amazing. He was the second MLB player to win Rookie of the Year and AL MVP in the same season. He followed it up with 10 consecutive Gold Glove Awards (2001–2010) for fielding and three Silver Slugger Awards.

Ichiro holds the MLB record for most hits in a single season. In 2004, he had 262 hits.

Giancarlo Stanton

New York Yankees outfielder Giancarlo Stanton led the National League in home runs in 2014 and 2017, has taken home two Silver Slugger Awards, was named NL MVP, and earned two Hank Aaron Awards for top hitter.

GLOSSARY

aluminum A silver metal that is strong and light

amateur Someone who does something without pay

bean To hit someone on the head with something

commissioner An official who is in charge of a professional sport

composite Made with layered materials such as carbon fiber

draft To choose people, one by one, for sports teams

dynasties Teams that are very powerful or successful for a long period of time

evolved Developed over time

front In a war, the area where opposing forces are fighting close together

Great Depression A time period during the 1930s when there was worldwide economic hardship. Many people lost their jobs and homes.

grounder A batted baseball that rolls or bounces along the ground

home run A hit in baseball that enables the batter to make a complete circuit of the bases and score a run

hybrid Something that is formed by combining two or more things

inducted Admitted or voted in as a new member

infamous Having a bad reputation

infielder Any of the four players who regularly play between the positions of first base and third base

ingrained Describing a belief that has existed for a long time and is difficult to change

inning A basic unit of play in which each team gets a turn batting

pastime An activity that is done for enjoyment

professional Someone who is paid for what he or she does

racism A belief that one race is superior; or hatred or discrimination based on race

reinstate To put someone back in a position or job that had been taken away

reserve To keep back or save for future use

retractable Able to be drawn back or back in

rivalry Competition between two people or teams to see which ones are the best

rookie A first-year player in a professional sport

segregated A forced separation of a group of people belonging to a different race, class, or ethnic group

settler A person who goes to live in a new place where there are usually few or no people

shortstop The player who defends the area between second and third base

standardized Made the same; made to agree with a model or rule

strike A pitch that is inside the strike zone or a pitch that a batter swings on and misses

wild card A team that has not won its division but has the best record of non-winners in its divison; this qualifies the team to play in the playoffs

LEARNING MORE

Check out these books and websites to learn more about baseball.

Books

Donnelly, Patrick. *Sports Illustrated Kids All-Pro Baseball Almanac.* Capstone Press, 2026.

Orrock, Anika. *The Incredible Women of the All-American Girls Professional Baseball League.* Chronicle Books, 2020.

Panchyk, Richard. *Baseball History for Kids: America at Bat from 1900 to Today.* Chicago Review Press, 2016.

Smith, Elliott. *Ballpark Legends: The Legacy of the Negro Leagues.* Lerner, 2025.

Websites

www.mlb.com
The MLB website provides information on all the MLB teams and players, along with stats, news, schedules, and more. Click on the players' links to learn all about your favorites!

www.baseballhall.org
The Baseball Hall of Fame has information about the history of baseball and the best baseball players of the past.

kids.britannica.com/kids/article/baseball/352829
Provides a comprehensive overview of the game, including history and rules.

INDEX